BRILLIONAIRE
THE POETIC PHILOSOPHER

Gotham Books

30 N Gould St.
Ste. 20820, Sheridan, WY 82801
https://gothambooksinc.com/

Phone: 1 (307) 464-7800

© 2023 *Dorian Mulder.* All rights reserved.

No part of this book may be reproduced, stored in a retrieval system, or transmitted by any means without the written permission of the author.

Published by Gotham Books (June 10, 2023)

ISBN: 979-8-88775-250-1 (P)
ISBN: 979-8-88775-251-8 (E)

Because of the dynamic nature of the Internet, any web addresses or links contained in this book may have changed since publication and may no longer be valid.

The views expressed in this work are solely those of the author and do not necessarily reflect the views of the publisher, and the publisher hereby disclaims any responsibility for them.

"Into emptiness"

Cautious of what's possible blood shed leaves a stain crutches then a cane victimize as a teen ' a broken femur by a pull of a trigger disregarded the significance I was swallowed into the emptiness Calamity dwells in the mind Soon enough the sequel arrives I made a brilliant mistake and fell into the trap,6 bullets with my name engraved body stretched out on the pavement. Death has a natural fragrance & nirvana has no odor, no sound, no feeling I became numb gazing into the emptiness.

"Unconditional Love"

Unconditional love requires the quality of mindfulness , it generates the power of awareness , it gives us the ability to look deeply into the nature of our own suffering causing us to reflect & understand unconditional love begins with us embracing the roots of our anger & accepting our misfortune not letting life harden our hearts . we must love ourselves First unconditionally meaning under any condition even through the cruelest circumstances then we will truly unconditionally love one another when we are aligned with a hearts, it will alleviate suffering.

"The cross roads"

    The cross Roads are a natural element of the obstacles we face on our Journey a pivotal time of meaning that becomes a result of consequences, which you may redeem conflict or prosperity caused by a Sufficient or inadequate decision we must weigh the potential reward of triumph and likelihood of failure to value the rational option applying a wise contribution to our lives or the lives of others cross Roads are perpetual a way of life It's not about avoiding cross Roads but become mindful of the symbolic revelations that present them Selves during times of enlightenment to prepare for our judgments at the cross roads.

"Still I will"

You may taunt & want to Kill me with your weapons of mass destruction you may follow
& plot on me right under my nose adding Insult to injury but still I will always rise

Does my arrogance disturb you? why are you beset with the blue's? cause I walk with my head high like I've founded Amazon

Just like good & bad
with the certainty of Conseque Just like cake in the oven Still I will always rise .

Did you want to see me perish? Body limp & a toe with tag Bleeding out like a women's menstrual weakened by my Sorrowful cries

Does my nobleness baffle you? Don't you make it awfully noticeable Cause I taunt you like Muhammad Ali down goes fraizer

You may creep when I'm sleep You may treason me with your fraternity.

you may kill me with your spitefulness but still I will always rise

Does my ambitions disturb you? Does it come as an amazement that I'm still alive to strive and persevere through adversity to beat the odds

out of the hospital with no shame I rise.

up from my death bed in pain.
I rise.

I'm a black philanthropist providing to the community maintaining & campaigning.

Leaving behind nights of ptsd & Paranoia I rise

into mindfulness I internalize wondrously I rise
I'm the dream of martin Luther king as I bear the gifs of my ancestors hope driven by their essence I rise , I rise , I rise Still I will Still.

"How to see"

Real eyes realize real lies , you must depict the truth , how can we when it Seems so Far Fetched , uncertain of the truth let alone a lie , Stuck between a hard place & a rock , how , when or where I have concluded for an individual to obtain the clarity through their vision needs to learn , unlearn , & relearn which will give yo the ability to realize real lies through real eyes

"Conquered love"

The love was once Superior as it reign royalty the gun chambered dishonesty discharging the First round piercing through the armor of loyalty which began the extermination the beginning of conquered love the battle was losed but the war was still to be fought the insufficient affection became infectious surely a biological weapon She said she understood his pain but lacked empathy clearly there was no remorse as she continued to Finalize the assassination with an arrow through his heart that hadn't belonged to cupid but conquered love

"Infinite Transformation"

    Day light Sunshines. Night time moon lights Seasons change approximately quarterly girls transform into women boys grow to be men . first puberty, then maturity global warming equals Climate change mariges & last names Happy men & women convert into transgender elementary to Jr. high , high school to college , Amateur then the pros make to the playoffs win the championship enter the super bowl ,gas operated automobiles turn into a fleet of electrical cars the world evolves there's infinite transformation

"Shadows Creep"

    The Shadows are near, can you see them, they just appeared silent but I can hear the whispers flow & enter my ear Shadows Creep when I'm sleep Awakening my 6 sense noticing my awareness they become elusive shape shifting but yet they don't disappear apparently they want my undivided attention the voices throw themselves across the room their silent but I can hear them vividly & clear the Shadows become bold making their presence known the shadows creep letting me know their consciousness is everywhere every time they appear.

"Love affairs"

Love can be sweet , love can also cheat Love don't cost a thing although love can cost Love everything, love why are you vulnerable can you hear my plea, love wants to be free a blue Jay that spreads its wings Love has its own pulse you can hear it beat Love may need to rest can you let it Sleep Love why do you make us weak but yet our strength is derived from your existence love is an emotion that can bring you to your highest peak or your lowest depth Love can be sweet.
    Love can also cheat. Love is alive but traumatized symptoms of post-traumatic stress disorder. Love is therapeutic. It is a remedy of holistic health love wants to be free a blue that spreads its wings.

"Perhaps"

Perhaps your love is tainted & your heart is contained with natural Sorrow perhaps your full of emptiness an emotionless hollow however your pain is a disastrous Melody have a chill pill perhaps your tense gets comfortable & reform your mood swings their relatively to misery you express grief much deeper than me. the depth of your soul your demon sleeps awaken by your saboteur Capabilities perhaps one day you're going to Self-destruct & blow up perhaps your anger provokes you to antagonize apparently you're a piece of diablo deceived & sabotaged.

"Define who?"

They, who, them, those people, you know the ones who would love to define you. How could they label you easily when they preconceive, I can't fit that jacket, nor will I wear it. Don't judge me, who? you. I could sue for character deformation, who you, Don't slander my name & try to define me , only God can judge me, those fools , who , them, you know the bias ones those fools who categorized you remember your future depends on, define yourself build character through righteously decisive choices.

"Misery Loves Company"

Do not entertain misery , it seeks out someone to gain attention & absorb ones positive energy to transition their state of mind into anger Sadness & Pity , Misery loves company it will sneak & Slily Find a host , misery comes in the Form of someone who calls you their friend even your relatives they will tell you they love but Fuel you with hatred awakening Self-deception forgetting who You are transforming your tender heart into rage you become misery needing company you now exist in the danger zone you're the devil's advocate the serpent who slithers on the surface.

"Broken Hearts"

    Healing a broken heart takes patience, it is a spiritual surgical procedure we must operate on , using the tool of Forgiveness seizing the vulnerable moments in our lives when we succumb to hatred , Fear , & Sadness this creates anger in the vessels of our broken heart , awakening our enlightenment that's deeply within , we become aware of our inadequacy confusion , resentment & blame . we learn how to correct our Flaws & unveil the hardness of the armor that covers our tender hearts letting love inject us with the antidote Joy that gives us the energy to rejoice & overcome turmoil.

"Will I Ever Trust Again "

    Will I ever trust again the pain of past traumas has me stressed Skeptical , everyone is suspect without acting suspicious I continue to be unhappy with the world around me it is the natural human condition when one has been betrayed shot in the back & I'm speaking literally it was too close to home it was a mental , emotional & spiritual transformation people say the world is corrupt but forget to realize they mean the people who inhabit the world will I ever trust again Knowing there isn't a such thing as being safe it's left up to us to be careful & aware of our surroundings.

"Death"

I welcome death for it is inevitable. Do I mourn over the dead? I am Spiritually Awaken my sorrow dies. It hurts for me to cry instead I celebrate the dead & disregard mourning . I've experienced near death tragically. I been to the ICU , I won't say I don't Fear death because I do we don't plan to die but it can happen abruptly & that's what I'm afraid of Death is just around the corner so I prepare For the worst I welcome death & adapt a healthy way of life in order to prolong death to live an extensive life I know i will surely die which is the reason I welcome death I won't be waiting on my time but rejoicing until my time.

"A Grandfathers Heart"

A Grandfathers heart that has infinite love such as yours should be nurtured & protected. A man of unconditional Love & understanding leads the blind in the right direction for thou shall not work with deception. The Kindness of a Grandfather's heart of infinite love shall not be taken For weakness. You gave me the greatest gift I could ever receive in which you lectured me until I respected the bigger perception, taught me how to view life experience from different angles . Brought me to understand common sense in which it is not so common to others you gave me logic in which I reason with life. Through you God spoke unto me for that I am truly blessed with the knowledge of a Scholar. It is only right that I genuinely express my gratitude towards you . You have set the bar, I wonder if I could ever become half the man you are . All in all I give credit where its due, no matter what I can never Forget about you . You made a positive impact in my life now It's left up to me to become who I am destine to be.

"O.R.(Operation Room)"

How would the Scalpel Feel if I wasn't unconscious , the sharp blade slicing through my delicate Skin , creating an opening where my organs are concealed . It still amazes me how the sedatives Keep my pain receptors sleep throughout the process of the operation . So many times, I Fantasize of feelings I will never Feel But who in the hell in their right mind wants to Feel the Surgeons hands in the operation Room I've spoken Figuratively an not literally only because I know I would Surely die from the pain alone of how the Scalpel would Feel.

"Better Than Some, Worster Than Others"

They ask your how are you , truth be told Better than some worster than others . Different strokes for different Folks, Hummpty dumpty Fell off -the wall & cracked his skull while bill cosby was charged with different counts of sexual assault . Don't let what you don't have hinder you continue to pursue happiness despite the struggles you will overcome the obstacles your main problem is that your stuck on stupid you doing worster than Some But Forget you doing Better than others Just remember to count your blessings & Stay under control.

"Starry sky"

At one with the imperishable stars Surpassing the clouds I can hear Gods accord welcoming me into the Divine kingdom his love resonates I've Ascended to the heights of his frequency displaying my reverence with gratitude for his salvation the infinite potential I will reach you can never Rob me of the light inside out I am the light At one with the imperishable stars I resemble the light house at Shore I shine through horrible storms I am the Starry sky.

"Capture"

Cultivating the beauty in each moment even when things get real ugly , through my lens I capture the integrity of my being I'm at peace the anger , pain & hatred has been deceased the struggle was real I was living on the streets I had to defend my morals the devil came in many forms I had a spiritual awakening I spoke to the divine I'm no longer divided I'm authentic pretend never me I capture the vision it was a prophesy the truth was revealed I'm consciously aware I'm properly prepared no priest but I preach Greatness optimism shall prevail when I stumble & fail I activate my resilience persevering through Misfortunes capturing the bigger picture and the Silhouette. I decipher the truth I'm a 100 % proof.

"Internalizing Positive"

Foster positive experiences, smile at those who smile laugh with those who laugh become a bundle of joy embodying optimism recapture happy times internalizing the positive recollection Savoring the experiences you most enjoy nourishing well-being & wholeheartedness replacing old pains with new & existing memorable moments Developing liberating insight will direct you on a path of awakening to be conscious of cause & effect you increase mindful Awareness enriching a success life.

"Light of Ascension"

Climbing the heights of the universe to unite with the spirit of the cosmos to become whole on a higher plane reaching the pinnacle of my mortal shell Similar to a butterfly in its Cocoon I'm waiting to metamorph by the OF Ascension entering Zion as a celestial being walking amongst the creator our father Awaken your Divine potential here on earth Abide by the law of cosmology to align Your Spirits Abode with the cosmic order Ma'at the divine truth.

"Shallow Hearts"

Deep as the Grand canyon my heart sinks, my heart lays at the bottom of the pit. Shallow hearts believe there higher as they look over the cliff but they Forget the higher they go the thinner the air gets. I've reached the clepths were pressure creates diamonds , I become meaningful with substance , they will never understand & welcome a caring hand only because the mechanics of a shallow heart cannot value the depth of empathy where I exist , their circuit boards are designed to work like this programed by the government to be slaves of their unconsciousness equivalent but not quite a machine I Call that a shallow heart.

"Divine Nightmare (Day I got gun down) "

Death was awaiting & my ticket was called in that moment everything went Dark until I realized the brightest light I had ever seen like it belong to an atomic bomb but it wasn't in arms reach it slithered through the end of the tunnel I could Feel the Divine casting over the nightmare and that's when all hell broke loose in an effort to Capture my soul I Felt reassured an became Fearless as I narrow my vision through the blur the intelligent light spoke I suddenly became receptive aware of telepathy understood the communication & began to control my breathing in that instant I awoke in John Muir hospital.

"Tearless Eyes"

Where do I begin does it ever end , timeless , life is deserted I can't even Feel the wind How do I manage to shed a tear through a pair of Tearless Eyes , I am so numb my soul is blind how will I ever reach my destiny when Soul Searching doesn't exist with me , where is the light that use to Shine so bright does God have a plan for me am I welcome to a kingdom of eternity , is there really a such thing of an immortal Soul if So why has the darkness covered the sky completely leaving no traces of the moon with neither the stars they Vanished too , if I could feel I would be severely hurting , I am So Faithless but Somehow I manage to shed a tear.

"The Noble Man"

The noble man will exuberantly respect his fellowship, exhibiting gravely qualities , humble with boundaries guided by discipline , debonair resulting to common Courtesy Staying in control presenting his poker face no one knows exist Have you met a man who treats his fellowship equally Superior without flamboyancy The conduct of the noble man is reserved no flamboyance , A Supreme being of moderation who's committed to excellence his integrity rest at the pinnacle of greatness.

"We Are Always in Transition "

    Moment to moment life is always changing, we have to accept that Life is impermanent we are always in transition • Once we can relax & understand every cell in our body is continuously changing we nurture the Flexibility of our minds & deactivate our Stubborn characteristics to embrace adaptability & acknowledge we are always in transition it motivates us to stop resisting against the nature of reality.

"How Can I Promise "

I am a man of my word but how can I promise when tomorrow isn't promised, my life can be taken away from me at any moment . I want to reassure you & comfort you but I will not promise you For I do not want to lie to you. I want you to understand I am a man of my Word So I will do everything in my power to gain trust & show you I am reliable, How can I promise when Death is anly promised.

"You Are A Queen"

He uses his charm to get beneath your skin, you're his prey and he is the predator his words flow & penetrates your ears he tells you exactly what you want to hear , it's your duty to differentiate the genuine from the wrongful manipulation can you recognize the truth or are you gullible . you're a queen, accept only a king, love who you are conquer low self-esteem.

"Am & Right"

You know it all !! Where do we begin?? I'm assuming you were.
going to say the book of Genesis!? ! How can we be certain? All that I learned is that I know is nothing . no one wants to be wrong , But we all failed . Am I right?

"I'm not in search of a soul mate"

I rather love then to be in love. I'm not in search of a soul mate instead I look to relate with a woman of harmony that can maintain the energy of compassion . My heart yearns to trust again someone to confide in. I'm not in search of a soul mate but if it is bestowed upon me I will embrace what has come to me & cherish every moment as if tomorrow didn't exist whoever she maybe I would love dearly an consistently.

"I am truly sorry"

IF I have broken your heart an ripped it apart understand I'm not a perfect man I know I have caused pain & Sorrow you grieve to me many occasions & I am truly sorry but today I am a better man I understand its hard to trust again I've pursued to be a friend & my love has always been genuine can you respect my hearts intentions & Forgive my imperfection you deserve tender love your heart is fragile I intend to redeem myself & treasure you as my queen if were destined to be then that moment ill Seize.

"I am a Warrior"

    I am a warrior of meditation, loving - Kindness, compassion & Joy the practices of Buddha, I train to acquire peace that deeply resides within to conquer hatred & abolish fear to relieve me of Suffering I am a warrior of non-aggression I Fight to overcome challenging Situations I am my own enemy Fighting the transitions of everyday struggles & negativity of other beings to create harmony with my peers & elders I am a warrior who Kills adversity with the enlightened heart.

"A Friend Like You"

    My heart yearns for a friend like you I imagine the collage we could create a master piece I've met no one like you in our galaxy you're surely unique. Time can only tell, what a Friendship like yours could bring, embracing a friend like you Someone I can confide in during a crisis a shoulder to cry on when life unveils tragedy you are incredible to say the least you're the one I Know that will understand my complexity your womany intuition & your wise Foresight should be nurtured by a Friend like me your beauty attracts the eye but your personality captures the heart. All I'm asking for is a genuine Friendship & unconditional love A mutual boud that despise greed this is my way of planting our seed I'll be the one who will appreciate your existence I don't mean to be sentimental it's just that my near death experience taught me to invest in a Friend like you.

"Infinity & Beyond"

We could do anything when we put our minds to it . This statement might Sound cliche, but it is a Fundamental Fact we should have learned when we were kids. Setting boundaries will only limit our Success & deny who we could become, we have unlimited potential Infiniti & beyond. I'm going to pursue beyond infinity wherever that may lead me to, realistically I'm taken Step For Step in order for me to walk. I haven't began to Climb but when I do I'll never reach a peak, have faith in all that you do & want to pursue it mind over matter & that's the truth.

"Hoodlum"

Life through the hoodlums eyes would scare straight a perpetrators facade poverty, murder, and violence. The havoc of the inner city is constantly yearning philanthropy life through the hoodlums eyes is vigilant paranoid of illicit crimes , Assault with deadly weapons , 211s , home invasions, car Jacking & Kidnaping poverty Supporting Genocide Jobless Hoodlums taking advantage of crimes to generate income to support their family habits & Fads.

"Old Soul"

From the consciousness of my mind to the depths of my Soul wise beyond the age 26 I reflect on cause & effect diligent & affectionate philosopher , a self-educated Scholar of the world learning through my own curriculum & life's experiences.

"Crystal clear"

I'm lost in the Fog I can't see I'm like a whale washed up on the beach Foreign to the land quite the contrary to a crystal ball I have no psychic ability despite my intuition the Fog has become a Liability I am not able to see crystal clear I lack Sufficient clarity.

"Psychotic"

The mind has a thin line between Sane & insane who's to say you won't become psychotic especially if you endure trauma the others are unfortunate they have been born with birth defects.

"Becon of light Illumination"

Shinning like a north star giving you a sense of Direction I'll guide you with insight & enlightenment to make sure you're well informed Illumination A Becon of light you can see me when the weather is real ugly & the fog is real low I glow in the dark I'm reminded of the moon.

I won't lead you astray or guide you the wrong way. I'm the light house at Shore Surely an Illumination a becon of light Full of intellect others call me bright indeed I am you can find me in the Starry night .

"Patience is a virtue"

I Feel jittery I can't wait , my anxiety has affected my nerves, my body Shivers & my stomach quivers & my heart rate increases pace. Patients is a virtue we all should cherish I encourage you.

"Follow the Rhythm within your heart"

Trust isn't given away For Free!!! It is Sacred. It is purchased with our honesty. They say blood is thicker than water But they spoke Figuratively Your blood relatives can cut you deeper than the white meat, Respect an unconditional bond you can Feel the trust in the depths of your Fragile heart . Follow the rhythm within your heart it will guide you away from those who are corrupt.

"Live like there's no tomorrow"

Enjoy life , live like there's no tomorrow , praise god , repent like there's no tomorrow, love your Family , Be Family oriented like there's no tomorrow , Experience different Foods like there's no tomorrow , party hard rock on , like there's no tomorrow , you never know what's missed until its gone , rekindle relationships like there's no tomorrow , Be humble , love yourself like there's no tomorrow , Show gratitude no attitudes like there's no tomorrow.

"The sun is born again"

I can feel the vibe. as the sun resonates
Peace comfort & Power
I bask in the essence of the
gigantic star mairinating the
summer's heat I embrace the
sun rise like a muslim during
prayer I enjoy the Sunrise as I
call it the birth of every day.
It's beauty radiates UV a powerful Frequency I absorb I am one with the Sun I am full of energy and I've reached my Pinnacle I like the Sun waiting to be born again.

"A lesson & a blessing"

You Fail, now you're discouraged. Do you let your Failure overcome you? I know it can knock you down but a winner is resilient you lost but don't be a sore loser, your adverity is a lesson & blessing. Reflect & correct your trials & tribulations A winner is a loser & a loser is a winner, Learn from your errors & elders . Terminate self-doubt without Faith you've already failed. Trust yourself in order to prevail.

"You are serene "

You're at peace within, your love radiates a powerful Source of energy as strong as the sun when one is near to you they can Feel the vibe of serenity through your frequency . Your heart is full of passion when you love you can hear a heart full of pain, it is the physics of serenity a spiritual medicine of holistic health you're serene.

"You were a Rose " (R.I.P Earllean aka grandma)

You were a rose, your love was tender but yet you were so strong you Fought the battle of cancer & overcame adversity . You were a reservist waiting on the war you encountered sorrow but replaced it with Smiles your strength alone kept you standing, nothing can come between us , you still exist in my heart your blood that pumps through my veins & your voice that echoes through my conscious mind reminding me not to take anything for granted you loved me unconditionally & pushed me to thrive. You were a rose & everyone knows to be careful of the thorns.

"Drown your Sorrows "

Your Sorrows Drown you & you drown your Sorrows life has afflicted you so you resort to drinking & Purchase a gallon of vodka You almost die From alcohol poisoning , So you Force yourself! to throw up , you yearn for affection that has yet to come . A Companion in the Darkness in the vulnerable night there is no Sun rise or sunset you acknowledge you are held captive by your mind. Free the caged Dove & utilize the expression of mind.

"The Caged Dove"

We must Find our courageous being that lies deeply within our core to free the caged Dove. During this process we acknowledge our insecurities that Fuels our Low Self-esteem. It is a transformative effect when we identify our sorrow, we awaken our courageous being. We Fight our Fears with compassionate mindfulness unblocking the delusion of our minds that once held us captive. We free the caged Dove, overcoming grief & hatred with gentleness & Forgiveness we learn to cope with the world & become less afraid to be conscious & Familiar of our suffering . Finding Liberty of conflict, we Free the caged dove.

"Thug Life"

I don't want to portray the thug life to the death of me or that will be the death of me I've grown to be a man . I stand for something so I won't Fall For anything . I changed my mentality for the greater good I want to live my life civilized , I ask god for forgiveness for For the sins I've committed , it was the rebirth of my heart & . the cleanse of my spirit you could call me Scary but the only thing I Fear is god , you pay the price with your life when You live a thing life.

"Born Into A world of Sin"

Born into a world of sin subject to the environment 1 resides in. The devil comes in the Form of our peers to entice the minds of the innocent to lead them astray on a dangerous path of unrighteousness committing misdemeanor & Felony crimes disregarding the 10 commandments we ignore all signs of God consuming mind altering drugs we ride the waves of the Frequency into a distant realm where we our taken out of our element Welcome to the depths of Lucifers Den Born into a I know world of sin.

"I know "

Doesn't it hurt? I know!!! How to cope? you plan a mass shooting & leave a Suicide note. Stop & put everything to a halt it won't work out for your best interest . God will Forever condemn your soul I know life has taken a toll, Be logical vs irrational its all psychological Find a way to express yourself in this cold world through a creative outlet or simply a demolition Job on a construction site find a social group who has endured pain in order for you to relate with others to learn a coping mechanism this is something I know.

"The Depression State"

The Darkness is where we hide in the time of distress we find the Coolness Soothing away from the sunlight we close the blinds in order to eliminate the natural light we Find comfort in Food , eating until we became obese , sleep is a Friendship we bond with in the depression state Drugs we abuse , Love we Defuse are minds become confused of our priority , Jobs are losed Friendships are broken , Family ties are ripped apart we do not participate with the world we remain lossed.

" A Motherless Child "

Where's the love A Deceased Father & a absent mother . She's so near but yet so far away. I accept the death of my Father but despise the existence of my mother I choose not to be cruel it's just she left me alone to deal with my sorrow when a child needs a mother's love The greatest pain has rested in my heart you try to teach me the essence of tough love , when will you ever Show Affectionate love & comfort your son your absence have affected me since day one . I love you more than words can express I could never welcome your death I may have said a word I regret but you have afflicted pain & those are the results that you get from the absent presence of a mother, I am a motherless child.

"Love Me"

You say you love me today , will you love me tomorrow if not I'll never dwell in the sorrow I'm sorry to say it my mother has already broken my heart I could never Let a woman bring me down I just want to know if you go be down for the ride when the struggles present themselves a Friend in the darkest hours we don't need to be in love Just as long as I know you love me genuinely & unconditionally I would be reassured you will love me tomorrow

"Heavenly Drafted (R.I.P. CHRISEAN NEALY) "

A young black teenaged , potential NBA 1st Draft pick A mistake that took him out the Game far worst then A torn ACL , A tragedy you can't recover from The Streets overcame chrisean hijacked of his innocence , A young black teenaged , potential 1st Draft pick thrived in sportsmanship as he carried his team to victory a leader an MVP on the court and a VIP off the court, a fun spirit , enthusiastic energy , & humorous personality I could only imagine A mothers grief tears of fire hard to sleep He lives through all of us (family) as long as you keep him alive in your mind you became conscious of his laugh out loud as the sounds echoes you could hear this the rhythm of dribble & the bass from his feet a song dedicated to Shante i would say R.I.P but He's more alive now then he's ever been he's not a point guard but our guardian Angel He walked through heaven gates GOD Drafted him VIP, MVP

"True beauty"

The color of my skin doesn't represent me. Although I'm judged by the complexion, I respect my origins considering the facts history has been stolen from the mother land black on black crime dominating the progress of the black community the ignorance of our beauty we disregard the true meaning of black pride I put my fist up in solidarity black live's matter when we are murdered by the white man but forget we participate in our own Genocicle and you wonder why I Stated the color of my skin doesn't represent me I have no shame of my rosts I'm trying to learn the culture now to shed off the ugly to radiate the true beauty of an African American.

"The Lonely Road "

Traveling down the lonely road where no one, not even your family considers your woes would they even understand if they welcomed empathy. Is it true that I'm alone to confront the lonely road the ear to confide in seems as if it doesn't exist I would cry amongst treasured Friends but I can't Identify who they are is it true that I have none not one I'm drowning in sorrow, can't swim. Have I gove unseen by the lifeguard o I hope to god I hate for this to be my Fate I have Sunken beneath the whorl pool I have to gather strength & build my farth on this lonely.

"Gentrification"

The sale prices of homes are doubling & tripling making it hard to own your own home, it has even grown difficult for people who earn low income wages to continue to pay rent in a 1 bedroom apartment causing homelessness the prices are ridiculous affecting neighborhoods Forcing tenants to live in other communities making their commute to Work Farther Gentrification changes a whole city providing homes for those who are making prevailing wages how can you be content making low income wages when gentrification is a common Fate Fueled with hidden hate it is a tragedy no one wants to Face in effort to make the city a better place to outcast those who fail to thrive & earn a sufficient pay check

"Live and let Live."

To just exist is a notion of meaningless no contribution to the world discover your purpose live a life of Significance making an impact in the lives around us a cause of righteousness learn what you have to offer time is of the essence set goals achieve goals become who you aspire to be internalize inspiration a transformation of interest . It is important to have self-awareness a mindfulness of relevance thrive with determination to prevail triumphantly live & let live.

"A Piece of heaven "

    A timeless bliss Surpassing any climax no drug can relate to a piece of heaven no words can equate a near death experience took me to the moon a weightless experience encounter A source of Freedom my emancipation of the restriction of my mortal shell feeling supernatural receiving extrasensory perception higher & higher I go traveling through black holes to different dimensions Farther & Farther I go to other galaxies I'm an extraterrestrial victimized Attempted murder cause me to Awaken my divine Potential I'm one with peace disconnected from my humanness Alleviating all suffering welcome to a piece of heaven.

"Infinite transformation "

    Day light Sunshines night time moon lights Seasons change approximately quarterly girls transform into women boys grow to be men first puberty then maturity global warming equals climate change mariges & lastnames Happy men & women convert into transgender elementary to Jr. high school to college Amateur, then the pros make to the play offs win the championship enter the super bowl gas operated automobiles turn into a fleet of electrical cars the world is full of transformation the world evolves there's infinite transformation.

"Love affairs"

Love can be sweet Love can also Cheat
Love don't cost a thing although love can cost you everything Love why are you vulnerable can you hear my plea Love wants to be free a blue Jay that spreads its wings Love has its own pulse you can hear it beat Love may need to rest can you let it Sleep Love why do you make me us weak but yet our strength is derived from your existence love is an emotion that can bring you to your highest peak or your lowest depth Love can be sweet , Love can also cheat love is alive but traumatized symptoms of post-traumatic stress disorder Love is therapeutic it is a remedy of holistic health love wants to be free a blue say that spreads its wings.

"The Buddhas refuge In God"

The awakened one by the immeasurable indestructible consciousness derived from the wholeness of being, Connected by Joy of enlightenment a natural state of felt oneness a vast dimension of love The buddhas refuge in God, the end of suffering the spark of luminosity timeless, deathless, bliss disposing incessant mental noise, you become a witness of thought, I am buddha the awakened one, reaching,

The liberational frequency of Gods refuge, I am being not human being The true nature that gives life to the physical body to disidentify from mind, name, & form will begin profound transformation, the radiant Joy of being the seed of enlightenment sprouts, you disenchant from defined Identity a realm of no mind not selfish but selfless, consciousness does not Need thought but thought cannot exist, without consciousness such knowledge is vital you become infinitely greater drawn to a new dimension of consciousness The Buddhas refuge in God.

"Take my hand"

How Sweet is Romance , will you take my hand & partake in this dance since love is a gamble are you willing to take this chance demolish the bitterness of past pain the struggles of a confined heart Soul search for your liberty , God's mercy is internal intimacy my love are rose pedals you can believe in me no fairy tale or fabrications my love is genuine & my character traits are Attentive a man of benevolence I won't promise my marriage vows , the romance of William Shakespeare is not guaranteed but I can reassure you Gods romance is sweet.

"BLACK XL"(excellence)

I say I'm black blakk & I'm proud I use to wear a nappy fro before if was in style blakk Xcellence never needed any clout born a Leader So I eliminate the peer pressure study the great so stagnation won't be my fate.

I'm a winner in the game F bomb a stalemate overcoming the winter storm in the summer time I use to be committed to crime now I Just shine I fell in line with blakk excellence tyler perry & oprah winery martin Luther King fought for are freedom of equality in order for us to have the opportunity to Succeed his work is my worth as a valuable asset BlACK XL .

"Hall of fame" (R.I.P MARLON EDWARDS)

You were loved by many & despised by plenty , who would deny your style like it wasn't trendy your presence demanded attention your heart showed genuine concern contributed to those around you . your love is not lost but the beginning of a new founded brotherhood you have been inducted to the brotherhood Hall a fame as you should can we all agree on one thing mardy was the heart of the party sincerity was Displayed through his Demeanor we won't miss you only because your being is whole through spirituality, guiding your relatives with Divine consciousness beware of his presence as they

Direct you through his intuitive enlightenment our compass when you may feel lost we know your are near. Let you bestow your gifts upon us even though we may not See the light although we may be in the Shadows you still encourage us when we are feeling sorrow we are all on borrowed time soon we will follow.

www.ingramcontent.com/pod-product-compliance
Lightning Source LLC
LaVergne TN
LVHW062000070526
838199LV00060B/4222